<u>ARE YOU READY?!</u>
SCREAM FROM ANGER!!!!

CRY FROM SADNESS????

OR WORK OUT YOUR WORRY?!?!

LIVE YOUR HAPPY!!

Time to Get It Out!!!

Section Mad

Time to talk about being MAD!!

Check out each question and write it out.

Now the real CHALLENGE: Can You talk it out?

Find your person and talk it through. It might still not go your way but at least you talked it out instead of bottled it up.

Look I'm Mad

You won't let me dress the way I want to!

_____

_____

_____

_____

_____

_____

_____

_____

Now can you talk about it?
If not, write why not.

_____

_____

_____

Look I'm Mad

When you don't see the good things about me!

_____

_____

_____

_____

_____

_____

_____

_____

Now can you talk about it? If not, write why not.

_____

_____

_____

Look I'm Mad

When you won't try some of the things I like!

_____

_____

_____

_____

_____

_____

_____

_____

Now can you talk about it? If not, write why not.

_____

_____

_____

Look I'm Mad

When you compare me to someone else!

_____

Now can you talk about it?
If not, write why not.

YOU'VE BEEN MAD!!!

TIME TO GET YOUR PERSON AND GO TO A GYM.
WHILE THERE, PUNCH OR RUN IT OUT!!

NOW, GO OUT TO EAT AND TALK ABOUT ANYTHING BUT NOT BEING MAD.

GOOD TALK?

Look I'm Mad

When you don't respect my time!

_____

_____

_____

_____

_____

_____

_____

_____

Now can you talk about it?
If not, write why not.

_____

_____

_____

Look I'm Mad

You push me too hard!

_____

_____

_____

_____

_____

_____

_____

_____

Now can you talk about it?
If not, write why not.

_____

_____

_____

Look I'm Mad

When you're too overprotective and don't let me live my life!

_____

_____

_____

_____

_____

_____

_____

_____

_____

Now can you talk about it? If not, write why not.

_____

_____

_____

Look I'm Mad

When you give me work at home after I've had a long day at school!

_____

_____

_____

_____

_____

_____

_____

_____

Now can you talk about it? If not, write why not.

_____

_____

_____

YOU'VE BEEN MAD!!!

TAKE YOUR PERSON, FIND A LOCAL MUSIC STUDIO, AND PAY FOR 1 HOUR.

RECORD YOUR SCREAMS, SHOUTS, AND YELLS ABOUT EVERYTHING YOU'RE MAD ABOUT WHILE YOUR PERSON LISTENS.

FEEL BETTER?

Look I'm Mad

When you punish me without hearing my side!

Dear _____

_____

_____

_____

_____

_____

_____

_____

_____

_____

Now can you talk about it?
If not, write why not.

_____

_____

_____

Look I'm Mad
When you make me do things because you think they're best!

Dear _____

_____

_____

_____

_____

_____

_____

_____

_____

Now can you talk about it?
If not, write why not.

_____

_____

_____

Look I'm Mad
When I feel like you just don't get me!

Dear _____

_____

_____

_____

_____

_____

_____

_____

_____

Now can you talk about it?
If not, write why not.

_____

_____

_____

Look I'm Mad

When you tell me I'm wrong about how I feel or what I think!

Dear
_____

_____
_____
_____
_____
_____
_____
_____
_____
_____

Now can you talk about it? If not, write why not.

_____
_____
_____

YOU'VE BEEN MAD!!!

CALL YOUR PERSON AND ARRANGE FOR THE LOUDEST PLAY LIST YOU CAN FIND.

NOW FIND A LARGE SPACE, CRANK UP THE MUSIC, AND DANCE IT OUT.

TIRED? GOOD. NOW SIT DOWN AND TALK IT ALL OUT. TALK THROUGH BEING MAD.

PAUSE PAGE

ANGER IS ONE OF THE STRONGEST EMOTIONS.

TIME FOR A PAUSE.

SO LET'S TAKE A BEAT. FOLLOW

BELOW TO REGROUP:

- SIT STRAIGHT IN A CHAIR.

- HANDS ON YOUR THIGHS AND RELAXED.

- BREATHING EVENLY, COUNT 5 ITEMS IN THE ROOM.

- TAKE A DEEP BREATH IN ... AND OUT.

- NOW COUNT 5 MORE ITEMS.

- TAKE A DEEP BREATH IN ... AND OUT.

GOOD, NOW LET'S GET BACK TO IT.

Section Sad

In this section :
Check out the questions
that make you sad!

Now the real
CHALLENGE:
Can You talk it out?

The Challenge is:
To try to talk it out with
your guardian to help them
understand what hurts
you.

We all feel sadness at
times. It is up to us to seek
help to cope with it.

Look I'm Sad
When you are too busy to be there.

Dear

_____

_____

_____

_____

_____

_____

_____

Now can you talk about it?
If not, write why not.

_____

_____

_____

Look I'm Sad
When you don't tell me you're proud of me.

Dear

_____

_____

_____

_____

_____

_____

_____

_____

Now can you talk about it?
If not, write why not.

_____

_____

_____

Look I'm Sad
When you're so busy working that you don't make time for me.

Dear _____

_____

_____

_____

_____

_____

_____

_____

Now can you talk about it?
If not, write why not.

_____

_____

_____

Look I'm Sad
When you wont listen to me.

Dear _____

_____

_____

_____

_____

_____

_____

_____

_____

Now can you talk about it?
If not, write why not.

_____

_____

_____

YOU'VE BEEN SAD!!!

FIND YOUR PERSON AND THE SADDEST MOVIE YOU CAN THINK OF.

NOW WITH A BOX OF TISSUE AND A BOWL OF POPCORN CRY IT OUT. EVERYTHING YOU FEEL WHILE WATCHING SAD SCENES FROM HOLLYWOOD.

FEEL BETTER?

Look I'm Sad

When you want to achieve your dreams through me.

Dear _____

_____

_____

_____

_____

_____

_____

_____

_____

Now can you talk about it? If not, write why not.

_____

_____

_____

Look I'm Sad
When you don't see I need help.

Dear _____

_____

_____

_____

_____

_____

_____

Now can you talk about it? If not, write why not.

_____

_____

_____

Look I'm Sad

When you don't see how hard I am working.

Dear _____

_____

_____

_____

_____

_____

_____

_____

_____

_____

Now can you talk about it?
If not, write why not.

_____

_____

Look I'm Sad

When you dismiss my feelings as unimportant.

Dear _____

_____

_____

_____

_____

_____

_____

_____

Now can you talk about it?
If not, write why not.

_____

_____

_____

YOU'VE BEEN SAD!!!

GO TO YOUR FAVORITE ICE CREAM SHOP OR DESSERT PLACE.

ORDER THE SWEETEST ITEMS ON THE MENU.

NOW EAT AND TALK IT OUT. ALL THE SADNESS YOU HAVE BEEN DEALING WITH.

FEEL BETTER?

Look I'm Sad

We don't have more fun or new experiences together.

Dear _____

_____

_____

_____

_____

_____

_____

_____

_____

Now can you talk about it? If not, write why not.

_____

_____

_____

Look I'm Sad
When I don't know how to ask for what I need.

Dear
_____
_____
_____
_____
_____
_____
_____
_____
_____
_____
_____
_____

Now can you talk about it?
If not, write why not.

_____
_____
_____

Look I'm Sad

When you tell me 'No' and I don't understand why.

Dear _____

_____

_____

_____

_____

_____

_____

_____

_____

_____

Now can you talk about it?
If not, write why not.

_____

_____

_____

Look I'm Sad

When I feel like I let you down.

Dear _____

_____

_____

_____

_____

_____

_____

_____

Now can you talk about it? If not, write why not.

_____

_____

_____

YOU'VE BEEN SAD!!!

TIME TO ENJOY THE OUTDOORS

FIND YOUR PERSON AND GRAB YOUR HIKING BOOTS, BIKES, WALKING SHOES, OR SPF.

NOW JUST ENJOY THE QUIET.
NO TALKING.

FEEL BETTER?

PAUSE PAGE

SADNESS IS INTENSE AND THAT IS OK.

TIME FOR A PAUSE.

FOLLOW BELOW TO REGROUP:

- LAY DOWN ON THE FLOOR OR BED.

- HANDS ON YOUR SIDES, PALMS UP.

- PUT ON SOME SOOTHING SOUNDS.
  - (LIKE RAIN, THE OCEAN, OR A FOREST)

- BREATHING EVENLY, CLOSE YOUR EYES.

- TAKE A DEEP BREATH IN... AND OUT.

- NOW CLOSE YOUR PALMS AS TIGHT AS YOU CAN.

- TAKE A DEEP BREATH IN... AND OUT.

- NOW OPEN YOUR PALMS AND EYES.

GOOD, NOW LET'S GET BACK TO IT.

Section Worried

In this section :
Check out the questions
that you are worried
about.

Now the real
CHALLENGE:
Can You talk it out?

This world is crazy and
continues to change
everyday.

We all feel worried about
the events around us.
It is up to us to seek help to
find comfort.

Look I'm Worried
When I'm not sure what is going to happen next.

Dear

_____

_____

_____

_____

_____

_____

_____

_____

_____

_____

_____

_____

_____

Now can you talk about it?
If not, write why not.

_____

_____

_____

Look I'm Worried

When I see on the news, that the world is not safe.

Dear _____

_____

_____

_____

_____

_____

_____

_____

_____

_____

Now can you talk about it? If not, write why not.

_____

_____

_____

Look I'm Worried

That I can't be good-looking without being taken for granted.

Dear
_____

_____

_____

_____

_____

_____

_____

_____

_____

_____

Now can you talk about it?
If not, write why not.

_____

_____

_____

Look I'm Worworried

That others won't get why I feel differently than they do.

Dear

_____

_____

_____

_____

_____

_____

_____

_____

_____

_____

Now can you talk about it? If not, write why not.

_____

_____

_____

YOU'VE BEEN WORRIED!!!

———

FIND YOUR PERSON AND GRAB A NEWSPAPER OR COMPUTER.

———

NOW READ SOME GOOD STORIES IN THE NEWS.

———

REMEMBER, FOR EVERY BAD STORY THERE IS A GOOD ONE.

———

HOW WAS IT?

Look I'm Worried

That I can't be myself without being bullied.

Dear

_____

_____

_____

_____

_____

_____

_____

_____

_____

_____

Now can you talk about it? If not, write why not.

_____

_____

_____

Look I'm Worried
When I think people won't give me a chance.

Dear

_____

_____

_____

_____

_____

_____

_____

_____

_____

_____

_____

Now can you talk about it?
If not, write why not.

_____

_____

_____

Look I'm Worried
When you don't see how much I need you.

Dear _____

_____

_____

_____

_____

_____

_____

_____

_____

_____

Now can you talk about it?
If not, write why not.

_____

_____

_____

Look I'm Worried

That I won't have your support if I'm not perfect.

Dear

_____

_____

_____

_____

_____

_____

_____

_____

_____

Now can you talk about it?
If not, write why not.

_____

_____

_____

YOU'VE BEEN WORRIED!!!

FIND AN ACTIVITY YOU ARE AFRAID TO TRY.

NOW FIND YOUR PERSON AND SIGN UP FOR IT.

SOMETIMES FACING OUR FEARS IS THE BEST WAY TO COMBAT OUR WORRIES.

FEEL BETTER?

Look I'm Worried

When you put too much on my plate, if I can handle it.

Dear

_____

_____

_____

_____

_____

_____

_____

_____

_____

Now can you talk about it? If not, write why not.

_____

_____

_____

Look I'm Worried

When you don't understand I need time to relax like you do.

Dear

_____

_____

_____

_____

_____

_____

_____

_____

_____

_____

_____

Now can you talk about it? If not, write why not.

_____

_____

_____

Look I'm Worried

That I don't understand the changes happening to me.

Dear _____

_____

_____

_____

_____

_____

_____

_____

_____

_____

Now can you talk about it?
If not, write why not.

_____

_____

_____

Look I'm Worried

You won't see me for me.

Dear

_____

_____

_____

_____

_____

_____

_____

_____

_____

_____

Now can you talk about it?
If not, write why not.

_____

_____

_____

YOU'VE BEEN WORRIED!!!

FIND A LOCAL CHARITY OR CAUSE.

NOW FIND YOUR PERSON AND SIGN UP FOR IT.

WHEN YOU ARE WORRIED ABOUT THE GOOD IN THE WORLD, BE THE GOOD THE WORLD NEEDS.

HOW DO YOU FEEL?

PAUSE PAGE

WORRY CAN HAVE US AFRAID TO LEAVE HOME.

TIME FOR A PAUSE.

FOLLOW BELOW TO REGROUP:

- CALL UP FAMILY AND/OR FRIENDS.
- GO TO A PARK, BOWLING ALLEY, OR SKATING RINK.
- NOW JUST SEE THE LIFE AROUND YOU.
- PLAY SOME GAMES.
- TAKE A MOMENT TO BE HAPPY IN THE ENERGY AROUND YOU.
- REMEMBER THAT LIVING IN THE MOMENT IS WHAT IT IS ALL ABOUT.

GOOD, NOW LET'S GET BACK TO IT.

Section **Happy**

In this section :
Ok, the negative is gone.
Time for the good stuff.

Now the real
CHALLENGE:
Can You talk it out?

The Challenge is:
There is something great to
find in every day.

Look around you. There is
good to be found and
enjoyed. Embrace it and
give the world that great
smile.

Look I'm Happy
When you see me for me and love me!

Dear _____

_____

_____

_____

_____

_____

_____

_____

_____

Now can you talk about it?
If not, write why not.

_____

_____

_____

Look I'm Happy
That you took me out to try something new!

Dear _____

_____

_____

_____

_____

_____

_____

_____

Now can you talk about it?
If not, write why not.

_____

_____

_____

Look I'm Happy
That today, I did something nice for myself!

Dear _____

_____

_____

_____

_____

_____

_____

_____

_____

Now can you talk about it?
If not, write why not.

_____

_____

_____

Look I'm Happy
That I'm wearing my favorite outfit and I look good!

Dear _____

_____

_____

_____

_____

_____

_____

_____

_____

Now can you talk about it?
If not, write why not.

_____

_____

_____

FEEL THE HAPPY!!!

WHAT IS YOUR FAVORITE ACTIVITY?

NOW FIND YOUR PERSON AND GO DO IT.

YOUR HAPPINESS CAN BE FOUND IN HAVING FUN DOING WHAT YOU LOVE.

DID YOU HAVE FUN?

Look I'm Happy
I got a great grade on my last assignment!

Dear _____

_____

_____

_____

_____

_____

_____

_____

_____

Now can you talk about it?
If not, write why not.

_____

_____

_____

Look I'm Happy
You told me you were proud of me!

Dear _____

_____

_____

_____

_____

_____

_____

_____

_____

_____

Now can you talk about it?
If not, write why not.

_____

_____

_____

Look I'm Happy
Someone complimented something about me!

_____

_____

_____

_____

_____

_____

_____

_____

_____

Now can you talk about it? If not, write why not.

_____

_____

_____

Look I'm Happy
I am on a great trip with my family or friends!

_____

_____

_____

_____

_____

_____

_____

_____

Now can you talk about it?
If not, write why not.

_____

_____

_____

FEEL THE HAPPY!!!

WHAT IS YOUR FAVORITE STORE?

NOW FIND YOUR PERSON AND GO SHOPPING.

SOME NEW CLOTHES, SHOES, AND BOOKS CAN HELP SELF CARE TO KEEP THE SMILES GOING.

HOW GREAT DO YOU LOOK?

Look I'm Happy
I helped someone today just to help them! It felt good!

_____

_____

_____

_____

_____

_____

_____

_____

Now can you talk about it? If not, write why not.

_____

_____

_____

Look I'm Happy
I just feel good today!

_____

_____

_____

_____

_____

_____

_____

_____

_____

Now can you talk about it?
If not, write why not.

_____

_____

_____

Look I'm Happy
Because I am around people who love me!

_____

_____

_____

_____

_____

_____

_____

_____

_____

Now can you talk about it? If not, write why not.

_____

_____

_____

Look I'm Happy
I realized a truth I like about myself today!

_____

_____

_____

_____

_____

_____

_____

_____

Now can you talk about it? If not, write why not.

_____

_____

_____

FEEL THE HAPPY!!!

WHAT IS A NEW ACTIVITY THAT WOULD MAKE YOU HAPPY AND YOU WANT TO TRY?

NOW FIND YOUR PERSON AND GO TRY IT.

TRYING NEW THINGS CAN BROADEN YOUR WORLD FOR THE BETTER

HOW WAS IT?

PAUSE PAGE

HAPPINESS IS A FEELING TO BE CHERISHED.

TIME TO REFLECT.

FOLLOW BELOW TO REMEMBER:

- THINK OF YOUR FAVORITE EXPERIENCES.
- THE ONES THAT REALLY LET YOUR LIGHT SHINE AND MADE YOU SMILE FROM EAR TO EAR.
- NOW GET YOUR CALENDAR AND MAKE SURE TO DO IT AT LEAST TWO A MONTH.
- MAKE IT A POINT TO CONTINUE SELF CARE AND HAVING EXPERIENCES THAT MAKE YOU HAPPY.

KEEP STRIVING FOR YOUR BEST LIFE!

WHATEVER IT IS YOU FEEL!! FEEL IT!!

YOUR FEELINGS MATTER AND NEED TO BE EXPLORED TO GROW.

TALK TO SOMEONE AND TELL THEM HOW YOU FEEL ANYTIME YOU NEED TO.

YOU ARE NEVER IN THE WAY OR A BOTHER SO SPEAK UP!!

WHAT ELSE DO YOU HAVE TO SAY?

Make sure you check out all this series journals from author
Glo Rose

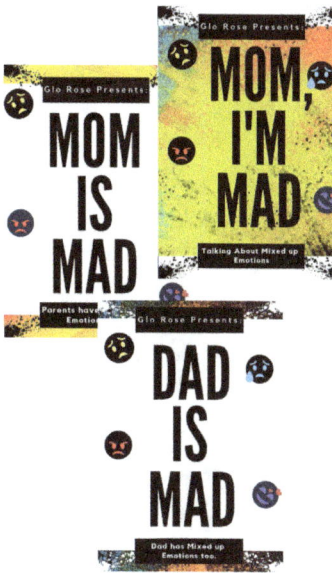

All are available at www.
GloRoseBooks.com

www.ingramcontent.com/pod-product-compliance
Lightning Source LLC
Chambersburg PA
CBHW061330120626
46546CB00007B/2747